The Best of Blaq Ice

A Look into My Thoughts

De'Andre Hawthorne

Inner Child Press, Ltd.

'building bridges of cultural understanding'

Credits

Author

De'Andre Hawthorne

Editor

hülya n. yılmaz, Ph.D.

Cover Design

De'Andre Hawthorne
Blaq Ice Productions
Inner Child Press International

General Information

The Best of Blaq Ice
A Look into My Thoughts

De'Andre Hawthorne

1st Edition: 2024

This publication is protected under Copyright Law as a "Collection." All rights for all submissions are retained by the individual author and/or artist. No part of this publication may be reproduced or transferred in any manner without the prior WRITTEN CONSENT of the "Material Owner" or its representative, Inner Child Press International. Any such violation infringes upon the creative and intellectual property of the owner, pursuant to International and Federal Copyright Law. Any queries pertaining to this "Collection" should be addressed to the Publisher of Record.

Publisher Information:

Inner Child Press International

www.innerchildpress.com

This Collection is protected under U.S. and International Copyright Laws.

Copyright © 2024: De'Andre Hawthorne

ISBN-13: 978-1-961498-38-9 (inner child press, ltd.)

$ 24.95

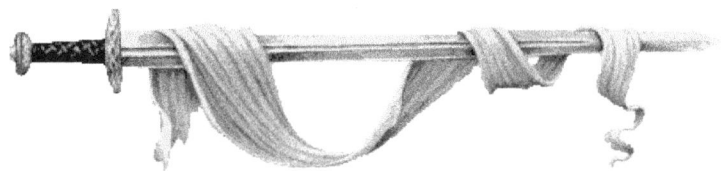

The Best of Blaq Ice is dedicated to those seeking daily inspiration. This poetic journey began as a personal challenge at the start of the year—to write at least one poem a day. The result is this collection, a reflection of my experiences over the past year.

I also dedicate this book to the poets who paved the way, laying the foundation upon which I now stand. To the voices that have passed but left an indelible mark on my life, like Strawberri Taylor, Mama Brenda, Mz. Conception, and Armen Rah—you remain an everlasting source of inspiration.

I thank the God of Abraham, Isaac, and Jacob for this gift, and my parents and family for their unwavering belief in me. My deepest gratitude goes to my children, the P.O.E.T. family, and all my supporters—your encouragement fuels my passion.

Preface

The Best of Blaq Ice emerged from a personal challenge I set for myself at the beginning of the year—to craft at least one poem every day. This goal was not merely about discipline; it was about capturing the essence of daily experiences and emotions as they unfolded throughout the year.

This collection represents more than just a series of poems; it is a reflection of my journey over the past twelve months, capturing the highs, lows, and everything in between. Each poem stands as a testament to the moments that shaped my days, offering insight and inspiration for those who seek it in their own lives.

As you journey through these pages, my hope is that you find not only a glimpse into my thoughts but also something that resonates with your own experiences, providing the daily inspiration we all sometimes need.

De'Andre Hawthorne

Foreword

The Best of Blaq Ice . . . A Look into My Thoughts is a scintillating social collection of consciousness by the award-winning poet/writer/organizer De'Andre Hawthorne. This publication presents a unique perspective on politics, love, and relationships, and most certainly offers the reader a glimpse into the soul of a man who has given everything to elevate culture and community.

This bold book is one of the author's many accomplishments, accumulated through poetry and spoken word, and cementing his international legacy in the art of language.

The author's impactful journey reflects a profound commitment to both the arts and civic engagement; as the Father of the Chicago Poet Laureate, he has not only elevated Chicago's literary scene but also shattered barriers as the first spoken word and hip-hop artist to run for political office in the city. His advocacy was instrumental in the renaming of Lake Shore Drive to Jean Baptiste Point DuSable Lake Shore Drive, a significant homage to Chicago's rich history, demonstrating how he has effectively turned his powerful words into tangible actions that resonate throughout the community.

Michael Guinn

Table of Contents

Preface — vii
Foreword — ix

The Poetry — 3

Why I Write	5
U Gotta Know	6
A Dream About 2 Kings	7
Celeste (Say Less)	9
This Week in the News	11
Time	14
Keep It Real	16
Just My 2 Cents	18
God Has a Plan	20
The Bulls Ring of Honor Celebration	22
Dedication	24
A Father's Sacrifice	26
It's Time to Do the Laundry	28
After Today	30
I Apologize	32
Forgiveness (Moving FWD Forever)	35
MLK Monday, 2024	37
Get Used 2 It!	39
When U Don't Feel Appreciated	41
Walkie Talkie	43

Table of Contents ... *continued*

Breathe	45
Agree 2 Disagree	47
Show Your Receipts	49
The Dash	51
I Have a Heart Problem	53
I Get the Picture	55
Don't U Ever . . .	56
The Damage Has Been Done	58
Above the Shoulders and Beneath the Waist	60
The Foul-Mouth Christian	62
We Celebrate U Today	64
That's My Cousin	65
A Moment 2 Remember	67
13 Years Ago, Today	70
Paisley Park	72
Celebrating a King	74
Why Is Our History Offensive?	77
Another Blessing	79
6 Is the Magic Number	81
The Grammys and Jigga	83
Black History Didn't Start with Slavery	85
The Royal Bloodline	86
This Dude Right Here	91
Who Rode the Redline?	93
Super Bowl 58 Highlights	95
Monday Morning Quarterback	97

Table of Contents . . . *continued*

The True Definition of Love	99
Making Noise in My Sleep	102
Between a Rock and a Hard Place	103
A Proper Salute	105

Picture Gallery — 109

Epilogue — 131

About De'Andre Hawthorne — 133

Web Links of the Author — 135

BlaqIce.com

The Best of Blaq Ice

A Look into My Thoughts

De'Andre Hawthorne

The Best of Blaq Ice

De'Andre Hawthorne

The Poetry

The Best of Blaq Ice

Why I Write

Something inside of me is burning
Yearning 2 be free
U can't cage a feeling or a thought
They both need 2 be released

I've been giving the world a small piece
Just a tip of the iceberg
Eyes have not seen, ears have not heard
Watch me turn these words 2 verbs

I speak life, words I manifest
If I've ever fallen short
Please forgive me, charge it 2 my head,
Not my chest

Besides the Sabbath
Ain't got time 4 no rest
I do what I gotta do
I ain't worried about the rest

Judge me on my works, Lord
I hope I've passed the test
Write me down in your book of life
Thank the Father that the Word was made flesh

My redeemer, my savior,
He gave me the gift 2 write these scrolls,
Anointed my pen and blessed my paper
Get this truth: hate me now, love me later

Because if expiration means death,
Then inspiration means life
I don't know why U do what U do
But this is WHY I WRITE

U Gotta Know

U gotta know that U are beautiful,
That U are unique, awesome
The fact that U are alive and well
And not in a coffin

Or coughing from COVID,
Making everyone around U nervous
Means U are blessed
U got 2 know that U are winning

God already knows the plans He has 4 U
And He knew it before your beginning
So, stand in your anointing,
Stop looking and pointing

Waiting on someone else
2 take the lead
Don't worry about what U are lacking
Have faith that God will provide all your needs

In Jesus' name
There's a price that comes with the riches, fame
And a household name

What does it profit a man 2 lose his soul
God is sufficient 4 U
U gotta know

A Dream About 2 Kings

Last night, I had a dream
About 2 KINGS
It was so unusual,
And as strange as it seemed

2 be having a dream about these 2 kings
I'm talking about 2 Kings
Who made such an impact
On the Chicago poetry scene

NICO and ARMEN RAH

Now, let me set up the scene

I'm in my hotel room
Deep asleep in my own little cocoon
In a whole other country
Somewhere in Mexico's Cancun

And these 2 KINGS entered into my spirit,
Invaded my thoughts
Amen Rah and I actually talked

And we were talking about
Going 2 see Nico who had just passed away
It was like a rerun stuck in my mind,
A flashback, or a replay

What is God trying 2 say?
What was my dream saying?
Lord, help me decipher the interpretation
These are the words I was praying

Later on, I saw Arnen Rah
He wasn't able 2 make it 2 Nico's services

So, I told him 2 meet me at the school
We had been sharing our poems
With young students, showing them that
Expressing themselves through poetry was cool

That was the last time I saw him
And spoke 2 him in my dream
He never made it 2 the school with me
2 mentor the teens

The next thing I remember
Was waking up from my dream
I looked at the time, and it was 7:19

Long live the spirit of these 2 KINGS
And everything they brought
2 the Chicago poetry scene

When I was penning this poem,
A light came on
Isn't it ironic, when U rearrange the name NICO,
Putting the I first and the N last, U get ICON?

TAP TAP TAP
Is my mic on?

Both of U left a legacy 4 future generations
U helped advance the art and moved the meter
I will never ever forget U 2 Kings
Nor will I let the poetry community forget U either

Celeste (Say Less)

I know a Queen
On the Chicago poetry scene
Who once told me something
That I will never forget

During this time, it was so chaotic
It was at the height of the resistance
Initially, not wanting 2 get involved,
She stood and watched from a distance

I still feel chills 2 this very day,
Thinking about the words she had 2 say
2 her brother

At that moment, she was in sync
She switched from sister and brother
And tapped into her motherly instinct

She was Sharon, I mean, sharing her thoughts
On a situation that disturbed her spirit
God sent her 2 me like Ananias was sent 2 Paul
2 remove the scales from his eyes

So that I could plainly see
See, I was just trying 2 be me
I wanted everyone around me 2 succeed
I wanted everyone around me 2 eat

But I learned that everyone
Can't sit at your table,
And U can't rationalize irrational minds
They are mentally unstable

But this Queen dropped something heavy on me
That weighed on my mind

She wrote these words and reminded me,
DON'T CAST YOUR PEARLS BEFORE THE SWINE

CELESTE (SAY LESS)

In other words, don't give what I value so much
2 those who don't appreciate me
She was referring 2 someone whom she saw me
Investing so much in,
And that person tried 2 destroy me

Til' this day,
I will never forget those 6 words
Thank U Queen, now I realize
There was a reason why all of this occurred

I definitely grew
Just know, U played a part in my journey,
And this poem was inspired by U

This Week in the News

2024 brought in some strange things
For poem 5 of 360 poems
I'm going 2 name a few things

First of all,
Big ups 2 Terrell and Cheryl from abc7chicago
Y'all put it down
I watched y'all NYE dance video
And y'all represented Chi-Town

At the time, I was celebrating
Teri Lyric Green-Manson's birthday
So, I watched it from out of town
But being from the windy city,
I can't lie, y'all made me proud

ABC even showed a dance video
Of me and my Queen
The first day of 2024 started off pretty good
Now, let me get down 2 business
And talk about these strange things

In just 4 days of this calendar year,
The news reports
That in the Chicago's west suburbs
2 women were shot and killed
One 19 and one 29, killed by a 21 year old
Jealous boyfriend, y'all young cats waaay too
Sensitive, stop popping them pills

And in Iowa, the news just broke
That a 6th grade student was killed
16 year old shoots up at Perry High School
One of the students told CNN, it doesn't feel real

The Best of Blaq Ice

Oh, and y'all better get up on these new laws
I stay in tune cause I'm curious
Did U hear about the new law in Illinois
Where workers get 40 hours of paid-leave time
In a 12-month period?

And New York Mayor Eric Adams was pissed
He's suing Texas 4 sending bus loads
Of hundreds of more migrants 2 New York
In other news, this was real wild
Did y'all see that brother in Las Vegas leaped over
The bench and attacked that judge in court?

I swear, he's wasting his talents
Trying 2 be hard and proving he ain't no punk
With those skills,
Dude could have competed in the Olympics,
Betcha he would've won the high jump

Who remembers Oscar Pistorious?
The track star with the prosthetic legs
A convicted murderer,
Who was found guilty of killing his wife
Talking about, he thought she was a burglar

Well, after only serving 9 years,
I can't believe he was released
We call it white justice because 9 years ago, I know
Black men who got more time 4 selling weed

Black social media complained about Color Purple
They say that Oprah messed it up
There was a little controversy surrounding it
When Taraji said she didn't get paid enough

And 2 close out this week,
Katt Williams went and lost his damn mind

De'Andre Hawthorne

He dissed Rickey Smiley, Kevin Hart,
Faizon Love, Cedric, and Steve Harvey all at the same time

Y'all think Katt's crazy, but he's a genius
This dude used his celebrity powers
Katt about to go on tour, he got hella promotion
He got 5 million views in 24 hours

This is just some of the news
And a tip of the iceberg
Maybe more people would be up on the news
If it was brought 2 U in Spoken Word

Who knows?
But stay informed, however U choose
This is King Of Poetry Blaq Ice signing off
With this week in the news

Time

Everyone gets the same amount of time
60 seconds for every minute
60 minutes for every hour
24 hours in one full day
Time is more than space, time is power

Time is valuable,
4 U can never replace it
Once U spend it or give it away
That's it, it's gone forever
So, please don't waste it

Treasure it, measure it
Equate it 2 your very life
If U wouldn't waste your life, don't waste your time
This is some of my greatest advices

Oh, and check this out
If U work for 8 hours and sleep for 8 hours
Spend 2 hours in traffic, eat breakfast, lunch and dinner
Bathe and shower

That's about 20 right there

How much time do U really have left?
3/4 of your life is taking every day
Just from the basics of life
Makes U wonder, what price do we really pay?

Just 2 live, so stay inspired,
Breathe life into the world,
Present yourself as a reasonable sacrifice,
Mentor some boys and girls

De'Andre Hawthorne

Stress 2 them the importance of time
How 2 protect their spirit and their mind
U can't undo what's already done
So, keep moving forward, never rewind

This is all a part of the science of time

Keep It Real

Reality, or so it seems,
Has been replaced by a false narrative
Social media has transformed society,
And it's imperative

That we keep it real
I've seen so many young people killed
Because of Facebook and tik tok posts
And don't let me talk about IG
They are on there doing the most

I've seen social media revolutionaries
That I've never seen at a rally or a march
I've seen high school dropouts,
Who all of sudden become conscious
And swear that they are smart

I've seen people get on live
And pour out their hearts
A whole lot of attention-seekers,
Who do this like it's an art

Tell a lie so good,
It's like they are painting a picture
Don't never go 2 church
But can tell U all about the scriptures

Fake photos and emojis,
Big girls with all face shots,
Pretending 2 be slim
Then go 2 their profile pic only 2 find
That the emoji looks better than them

If we can just be who we are
And stop pretending 2 be what we're not,
A lot of this nonsense that we see
Would surely stop

De'Andre Hawthorne

Just get in where U fit in
Folks gonna feel how they feel
Just be the best version of yourself
And most of all, keep it real

Just My 2 Cents

Let me give my perspective
On this issue concerning the migrants
There is a lot going on behind the scenes,
And I ain't buying in

We have a democratic administration
Who are permitting them 2 come
Yet the narrative is
It's the Republicans' fault, but I ain't dumb

White folks in power always do the math
They crunch the numbers,
They make moves behind the scenes
While the masses get dumber and dumber

The polls say that if the election was today,
Trump would beat Biden by a slight margin,
And in the words of Marvin
What's going on?

Then the light came on
Migrants are arriving by the thousands
They are receiving financial support,
Health care and housing

They've jumped ahead
of the legal citizenship line
2 qualify 4 naturalization
Wouldn't it be something,
if by the 2024 presidential election,
They are allowed 2 vote in this nation?

Hmmmmmmm, think about it!

Now on the other side of the isle,
Republicans peep game
Because every action requires a reaction,
And the right wing is like 2 can play that game

De'Andre Hawthorne

Since U are allowing them asylum
And don't want 2 protect our borders,
I'm going 2 flood all the democratic
sanctuary states with migrants,
And see if they can afford it

Afford 2 support these migrants with
Their state and local budgets
Now, the black and Hispanic voters are
Pissed off, saying this doesn't

Make sense, and U can't blame
Donald Trump and Mike Pence
They've found money, food and shelter
4 the migrants while our own homeless
Are sleeping outdoors in tents

All the financial help that they used 2 get
Is being cut back and cut off
The Republicans want U 2 blame these
democratic leaders and they are 2 fault

They know that U will never vote Republican
They just want U 2 stay at home
The Democrats are trying 2 create voters
While Republicans want Trump
Back on the throne

It's all one big political chess game,
And we are all pawns
Be aware, stay on guard,
Stay woke, this is your alarm

Let me know what U think
Let me know if this makes sense
This is King Of Poetry Blaq Ice signing off
This is just my 2 cents

God Has a Plan

I received some sad news today
It came in the format of a text
I mean, it was out of the blue,
A text that I didn't expect

It was a sister of one of my patients
She sent me a link 2 click on and play
She said, "I just wanted 2 thank U 4 taking care
Of my brother, but my brother passed away"

The link showed that it was yesterday
All I could do is pray
Lord, cover and comfort his family
Thank U 4 giving him peace
And taking all his suffering away

I remember when I first met him
He was at the hospital on 6 West
He was very uncomfortable
And really could get no rest

His sister Monica had some things
She wanted 2 get off her chest
She said that some of the nurses hadn't
Treated her brother right and giving their best

That's when I was asked 2 step in
We met as strangers
And soon became friends

I was able 2 help facilitate a few things
With the help of my leaders
I encouraged him in the name of Jesus
I could tell that he was a believer

De'Andre Hawthorne

I put posters on his wall; so, when he woke
He could see positive words and scriptures
The words were written in Spanish
So he could understand and clearly see the picture

God saves and God heals
God is present and God is real
There are some cups that we cannot pass
At the end of the day, God have your will

Although I am saddened by the news,
I have hope and faith in God
And 2 his big sister Monica,
I know this is going 2 be hard

Sometimes we may ask, why me?
Sickness and death are hard to understand
Just hold on 2 your faith and know
That God has a plan

The Bulls Ring of Honor Celebration

In just one day away from today,
The United Center will be on fire
Side note, LeBron ain't never THE GOAT
The devil is a liar

Ok, I'm back, whew
I just had 2 get that off my chest
There are a lot of greats out there
But there's only one who can be considered the best

I remember those championship years
Boy oh boy, Chicago was off the chain
Everyone in the world wore that #23 jersey
Everyone knew Jordan's name

But remember 72 to 10
The Bulls only had 10 losses and 72 wins
One of the greatest teams ever assembled
With 5 men (on a court)

Yea, I know what y'all thinking
The 2015 - 16, Steph and The Warriors beat that record
But I've got one better, don't trip
Not only did the 95 - 96 BULLS have 72 -10 wins
That same year, they won the championship

That's the difference, but listen
This Friday, we have a moment 2 thank the team
That gave us some of the best years of our lives
Moments these Lebron fans have never seen

THE HONOR OF RINGS
Will be celebrating some of the greatest
Players who have ever played
They took the game 2 another level
It was poetry in motion, smooth as ballet

De'Andre Hawthorne

I would personally like 2 say, thank U
Thank U 4 the memories, the hard work, and dedication
Join me as we celebrate with THE HONOR OF RINGS
And give them a standing ovation

Dedication

Every day, it's a struggle
Every day, it's a grind
It's like a race against the clock,
A race against time

This is enough 2 play tricks on your mind
Burdens, tossing and turning
Learning from your past
U remember what it was like 2 be hungry

I don't ever want 2 feel
That feeling anymore
So, I wake up every morning, 10 toes down
And when my feet hit the floor,

I'm running,
Not looking back
The only gear I know is drive
I'm moving forward with wind at my back

Despite the obstacles
And naysayers,
I get strength through God and prayer
This life comes in layers

New levels
And new levels come with new devils
But keep moving, losing is not an option
U are God's child, part of the adoption

So, even when U don't feel like it,
Keep going
Even when U want 2 stay where U are,
Keep growing

BE DEDICATED
That means, no matter what, U do it
The days U are tired and don't feel good,
Or don't want 2, U still do it

Because it must be done,
And who better 2 do it than U
Your grind has 2 become a part of U

A part of your DNA,
I'm talking about greatness in the making
But it all starts in your heart and mind
It all starts with dedication

A Father's Sacrifice

I remember my father
Always providing amd taking care of us
His CB handle was Hot Pepper
His profession was driving trucks

He took on the responsibility
Of taking care of 3 girls, 2 boys, and a wife
In the 60s and 70s
I can only imagine what life was like

We really didn't have a lot
But we had enough
Sometimes no heat
But there was always something 2 eat,
Even when times were rough

Daddy made it happen,
And he supported my dreams
Whether it was baseball or rappin'

I remember sneaking, showing my friends
His arsenal of guns,
Crossbows and rifles
We would hear someone coming and run

Those were the good Ole days
When times were fun,
Scraping up crums 2 make ends meet
We kept our faith in God, we believed

On Sundays, daddy watched TV
Until he dozed, he called it resting his eyes
Man, we watched westerns all day, Bonanza,
Gun Smoke, The RifleMan, and Rawhide

De'Andre Hawthorne

Rollin, Rollin, Rollin, lol
He would barbecue at our baseball games
Then at night, drink, listen 2 blues
While the family gambled playing card games

Budweiser and Philip Morris cigarettes,
Down home blues on 8-track cassettes
He always bought us Christmas toys
My favorite was the Dukes of Hazzard race track

And he would always
Dress 2 impress,
Cowboy boots, sometimes 3-piece-suits
Daddy was always dressed
My childhood was the best

Thanks 2 my father

Thank you for providing 4 me
And giving me life
Thank U 4 being an example of a man
There's nothing like a father's sacrifice

It's Time 2 Do the Laundry

Some say, it's a woman's intuition
Some call it suspicion
U can see a lot of things with your 3rd eye
As long as U pay attention

2 the signs,
Listen 2 that little voice in your mind,
Telling U that something is off
And people don't usually admit their faults
Until they're caught

But we all have 2 take some responsibility
We have the ability 2 accept or reject
Let our pride go, show some humility

So, today, I decided 2 do some laundry,
Separate the darks and whites
What's wrong and what's right
What we are willing 2 accept
Determines our quality of life

And I don't want 2 live in this space no more
So, it's time 2 do my chores
See, instead of a Queen, he preferred whores
Defiled my bed; so, I scrape the floors
With her nasty ass

Becky with the good hair,
U can have your affair
Unwanted guests when I'm not there,
Coming home from work early,
Just 2 see her there,
Like Goldilocks and the 3 bears

'Somebody's sleeping in my bed'
I tried my best 2 bust her head
2 the white meat
My black husband and my white sheets

De'Andre Hawthorne

It's time 4 me 2 do some laundry y'all,
Separate the darks from the whites
Because you're dirty and she's foul
U prefer a dope fiend over a wife

Well, I'm going 2 give U
Exactly what U deserve
I guess section 8, a place 2 stay,
And the bills being paid is not enough
I'm the breadwinner, boy, U got some nerve

See y'all, I had to clean my house
So I could get my life together,
Separate the whites from the darks
The dirty from the clean
Because I deserve better

2 my sisters,
It's important 2 protect your spirit,
Your heart, and your mind
Build your self-esteem, keep your faith
Trust me, you'll be fine

Because sometimes it's just
TIME 2 DO SOME LAUNDRY

After Today

How many times have U said 2 yourself,
"After today, I'm gonna start . . ."
Whatever it is,
We always disregard

The current situation
Have U ever heard the old saying,
"Why put off to tomorrow what U can do today"?
Yeah, I'm sure U have, but anyway

It's like we gotta get our minds right
Or battle a war from within,
And we must win the fight

Before we can start this new journey
Whether it be giving up something
Or losing weight,
It's like we gotta get that last piece of food
Off our plates

Then AFTER THAT,
Or even starting tomorrow
It never fails,
And we always seem 2 follow

This same formula, and I wonder why
Like if we knew we were going 2 die
Would we put it off until tomorrow
2 say our last goodbyes

The moral of the story is,
Don't none of us have time 2 waste
It's all mind over matter
On top of a little faith

De'Andre Hawthorne

So, let's replace AFTER TODAY
With starting right now,
And trust me, U will achieve your goal
Some way, somehow

Because I believe in U
And I'm proud of U
Just know and realize
There's nothing standing in your way but U

I Apologize

I apologize 2 everyone whose feelings I've hurt
My teenage years were something else
Lying 2 those girls 2 get what I wanted
I'm sorry, I was just exploring myself

I apologize 2 my parents
For being a disobedient child
Those times I didn't want 2 follow your rules
Running free and wild

But now, I really can understand
How much responsibility comes with
Being an adult; now that I'm a man

I APOLOGIZE

I apologize 2 my wife
God blessed me with U in my life
It's still a struggle trying 2 get it right
It's an everyday struggle and fight

I apologize 2 all my teachers
4 being rebellious and not focusing in class
I apologize 2 my rear end because Mr. Everret
Would get that paddle, make me roll the dice,
and wear out my ass

Whew wee! I felt like Denzel in *Glory*
During that whipping scene,
When he was trying not 2 cry
Just thinking about it right now
Is making tears well up in my eyes

I APOLOGIZE

De'Andre Hawthorne

I apologize 2 my sons
4 the sacrifices I had 2 make,
Working and hustling all day long,
Trying 2 keep food on your plate

I apologize 2 my first love
4 taking advantage of your love and loyalty
Physically, I may have strayed
But my heart has always stayed
I still get goosebumps when I hear your name, Poetry

So, in honor of U, I write
2 make sure your light still shines brightly in my life
You've given me an outlet 2 write my wrongs
So that I can right my wrongs

When I recite these poems,
It's like I transform
People see the anointing from God,
And the years of weathering the storms

SO, I APOLOGIZE

Last but not least, I apologize 2 God
This life is far from easy, it's been so hard,
Dealing with past traumas, cuts, and bruises,
Pulling off these scabs, reliving old scares

But God, U continue 2 do Your job
Showing grace and mercy,
You've covered me as far as I could remember
Since the days of Cotton Nursery

I've been shot at,
Almost strangled 2 death
And when I lost my son, I'm glad I didn't have a gun
Cause I felt like I didn't have nothing left

THAT'S WHY I APOLOGIZE

Because I've always had U
Even at times I took U for granted
Although U planted a spirit deep inside of me,
Gave me understanding of your word,
Unlocked my heart, so my mind can be free

I just hope that everyone I apologized 2
Can forgive me
Forgiveness is more about us and God
I definitely forgive those who wronged me

I APOLOGIZE

Forgiveness (Moving FWD Forever)

We all suffer from past hurts
And traumas
It's hard 2 heal from your past
When U relive it with everyday drama

Your mind just won't let U rest
It's like U have a million things
U need 2 get off your chest
But the test of life can be very heavy

And U carry around all this weight
Blood pressure rising,
U began 2 question your faith
So, U have some choices 2 make

Do U believe that God heals
And prayer changes things?
Can U lay it all on the altar of God
And stop trying 2 do God's job?

Oh, and forgiveness doesn't mean
That U have 2 let that person back in
It just means, let it go, stop talking about it,
Stop thinking about it, and giving it energy
This goes 4 family and so-called friends

Look, I know that you've been through
Some stormy weather,
But God wants U 2 forgive
And FORGIVENESS means
Moving FWD forever

Together, U and God can defeat anything
But U can't do it alone
No matter how much pride and ego U have
You'll soon find out, U are not that strong

No matter how much testosterone
Sometimes, only God can fix what's broke,
Stop stressing yourself with
Anxiety, high blood pressure, and strokes

Because U haven't learned the science of
FORGIVENESS (MOVING FWD FOREVER)

I'm not saying forgiveness
Happens all at once, it comes in layers
Just read those 2 little verses
Right after "The Lord's Prayer",

And trust
It says if we forgive men their trespasses,
Our Father in Heaven will forgive us

And if U are not willing 2 forgive,
Your Father in Heaven will not forgive U
I'm not telling U what I think
I'm telling U the truth

So, 4 your own benefit, find it in your heart
2 forgive those who hurt U
And moving forward, don't cast your pearls
Among swine, find someone worthy
2 give your heart 2

MLK Monday, 2024

On MLK MONDAY, the windchill was -20°
I awoke 2 some extreme weather
The day would soon become very interesting
I don't know if U could say, "better"

As I drove 2 work, the radio stations played
Speeches from Dr. Martin Luther King
From "If I Had Sneezed" 2 "I Have a Dream"
By the time I arrived at work, it was 7:18

The Chicago schools were closed
Because the temperature was too cold
Back in the day, I went 2 school in all types
Of weather. Man, I must be getting old

Meanwhile, Iowa spoke 2 the nation
In their Iowa Caucus' votes
It was the coldest Caucus in history
They stood in lines with their hats and coats

By the time their polls closed,
Donald Trump had won by a landslide
He won by 51% of the vote, never before
Had a candidate won by a margin so wide

It looks like, if Trump could stay out of jail,
He has a clear path
2 be the Republican nominee
And in NBA news, my Bulls lost 2 the Cavs

The 75th Emmy awards aired live on Fox
Congrats 2 those who took home awards
Anthony Anderson kicked it off, singing
Themes from all the old TV shows
They loved it, they all sang on one accord

The Best of Blaq Ice

It was accompanied by
The old-looking TV sets
But the best part of the night 4 me
Was seeing the legendary Carol Burnett

And on Monday Night Raw,
The championship match was a brawl
But Seth Freakin Rollins retained his title
Over The Modern Day Maharaja Jinder Mahal

And in the NFL, Monday Night Football
Aired live on prime time
The quarterback Baker Mayfield showed out
The Eagles beat the Buccaneers 32-9

Last but not least, I ended my night with my wife,
My lover and my best friend
We went 2 the movies 2 see the *Beekeeper*
It was so good that I would go see it again

This was my MLK MONDAY 2024
I hope y'all stay safe and warm
This is also poem number 17
Of 360 poems

Get Used 2 It!

Time brings forth change,
And sometimes change can appear 2 be strange
A new place, somewhere U have never been
A new U, a new mindset, and new friends

GET USED 2 IT!

Whether U like it or not,
It is inevitable, it will come
There will be nowhere 2 hide
And nowhere 2 run

GET USED 2 IT!

The sooner U embrace the fact
This is a better version of yourself,
That the old U don't work anymore,
Leave that old way of thinking on the shelf

GET USED 2 IT!

U can get through
What U are going through
U can heal from all the past hurts
But U have 2 want 2

U can get 2 the next level
Receive that promotion and achieve goals
U have much more inside of U 2 show
God has blessed U beyond measure
More than U know

So, be ready, be prepared
4 what's about 2 come

This is your moment, this is your time
Just acknowledge where the blessings
Come from

GET USED 2 IT!

Because starting today,
Your life will never be the same
I pray that God gives U more than U ask 4
In Jesus' name.

When U Don't Feel Appreciated

When U don't feel appreciated,
Don't Change
God sees what others don't
Even when others pour salt on your name

Some will bring up old issues,
Past mistakes, things that U used 2 do
They won't let U shed your cocoon
They hold on 2 the old U

Like Jacob held on 2 the Angel,
They pull out things in the past
U can do 100 things right and 1 thing wrong,
It's the 1 wrong thing that seems 2 last

It gets brought up every time
Someone says something good about U
As if 2 say, U are not who U appear 2 be
Now U have 2 prove that their point of view
Of U is not true

This is when U don't feel appreciated
But don't change, don't turn away
The good thing is what God has 4 U is 4 U
No one can take it away

See, U can give your all,
Go above and beyond the call of duty
Be there when needed, whenever U are called

And 2 some this is still not enough
But, God knows your heart
He sees the difference U make every day
Trust Him, He will make a way out of no way

Stay the course, U are doing a good job
And man may or may not give the award
Just make sure what U do
Is pleasing 2 God because He
Is the only one that gives the reward

Walkie Talkie

Have U ever known someone
Who U thought U could confide in,
Tell your innermost secrets 2,
Someone who U thought was your friend?

It could even be your next of kin
That's why God says
"Do not put your trust in men"

Believe me, the moment U share anything
With anyone, it's no longer a secret,
And if U don't want anyone else 2 know,
It's best 2 keep it 2 yourself

Because there are some WALKIE TALKIES
Out there who can't hold water,
And if U just gotta get it off your chest,
Go in that closet and talk 2 the Father

Everyone who U think has your best interest
At heart, really don't, they're just worthless
They point their fingers as if 2 say I told U so
Like your life is supposed 2 be perfect

Some of these same people U trust in
Gossip about other people 2 U,
And U know what they say, "those who gossip 2 U
Will gossip about U"

Those WALKIE TALKIES

And my sister Ro Ro
Is one of the biggest WALKIE TALKIEs I know
She's going 2 tell it

The Best of Blaq Ice

If I talk 2 her about something I'm going through, I know
That as soon as I hang up, and call my mom,
Before I can tell her about it, she already knows

Boy, she is faster than Xfinity Internet
Or T Mobile on 5G
Some of these people U tell your business 2
Will have your business all over the street

So, be very careful whom you confide in
They will look at U right in your face
Then talk about U behind your back,
And like butter, have your business spread
All over the place

Be wise, open your eyes
There's nothing wrong with talking 2 a shrink
Because at the end of the day, U have 2 be very selective
U can't talk 2 everyone about everything

Breathe

Take a moment 2 exhale
I'm sure if these walls could talk,
They would have some very interesting
Stories 2 tell

Now, inhale,
Breathe in the positivity,
Get rid of the negative people
And the toxicity

Some of these people out here
Are worse than poisonous snakes
It's time 4 U 2 let somethings go, move on
And clean the slate

Start from scratch,
Surround yourself with those who support U
Make sure their spirit matches yours
Get rid of all those miserable people,
Who see your joy and try 2 snatch yours

BREATHE

I know it's irritating
But don't be led by your emotions
What U need 2 do is focus on U
And stop focusing on them

The chances of them
Ever changing are slim
Don't let them take your bright light
And make it dim

Also, take some responsibility, and
Understand why U keep attracting

The Best of Blaq Ice

The same type of people
U don't want 2 accept the fact that U have
Something inside of U that's equal
Or in common with the one's
Whom U attract
Maybe they are showing U a mirror of a side
Of yourself, and U don't like that

But one day, U will have 2 face, and will
Make some personal character adjustments and replace it

With a better version of yourself
Then watch, U will start attracting people
Who really want 2 see U win
They will celebrate and applaud your victories
These will be your true friends

SO, BREATHE

Learn 2 love from a distance
Everyone isn't meant 2 be in your circle
Because it's only the people U let close 2 U
Who can really hurt U

Stop relying or depending on others
God will provide all that U need
Believe me, U only need the faith of a mustard seed
Sometimes U just have 2 take a moment
2 relax, and just breathe

De'Andre Hawthorne

Agree 2 Disagree

No 2 people were created the same
And if U think everyone is going 2
Agree with U, U must be insane

See, insanity is doing the same thang
But expecting a different result
U keep trying 2 win people over
But if 2 are not in agreement, can they walk?

Together, it could be
Your mother or your brother
They damn near can't even
Have a conversation and talk to one another

Without there being some type of argument
See, it's better 2 keep peace
And sometimes,
U just have 2 agree 2 disagree

Is it that important 2 win an argument?
Is it that important 2 prove U are right?
Now, your wife is all upset
And U can't get none at night

And U know what they say
"Happy wife, happy life"
Now, U gotta make things right

The morale of the story is
Sometimes U have 2 take a step back
Especially when U are in your feelings,
It's all in the way U react

And at the end of the day,
It's all about respect

The Best of Blaq Ice

Maybe God has revealed some things 2 U
That He hasn't shown them yet

But never forget
When U were blind and dumb,
Others would try 2 enlighten U
And U couldn't understand
Where they were coming from

Give that same person
That same patience others gave U,
And stop acting like U always knew
The things U know now because once upon
A time, U didn't have a clue

Until God worked on U
And opened your eyes so U could see
All I'm saying is, sometimes 2 keep peace
U have 2 agree 2 disagree

Show Your Receipts

Have U ever left the store with a grocery cart
Full of items, and right before U leave
Out the door, U had 2 show your receipt?

Sometimes people don't believe
U are who U say U are
That U are not up 2 par
That U are trying 2 be something U are not

In a world full of avatars,
Fake profiles, internet stars,
Air BNBs, and rented luxury cars,
It's all a big facade

I'm telling y'all, today,
U can't even recognize
The real from the fake

U gotta show receipts

Then there are the doubters, the naysayers
They see U winning, U show receipts
And they're 2 busy waiting on your downfall
They don't know, U reap

What U sow, so show your victories,
Tag everybody in your network,
Show your receipts. U are really doing it
They're watching so hard their neck hurts

See, receipts go both ways
Proof 4 others and satisfaction 4 U
Knowing that U worked hard
And paid your dues

The Best of Blaq Ice

In the hood, we say,
"Keep doing what U do"
U may not think that people are watching
Post a story, and U can see who views

Just in case U haven't heard it in a minute,
I'm proud of U and I believe
U are everything I see U 2 be
U have shown me your receipts

The Dash

This life we live is so finite
When U consider how long the sun, moon,
And stars have been around compared
2 human life, it gives U a different insight

Rocks, rivers, and seas
Mountains, canyons, and trees
They make me think why am I so important,
What God sees in me

Maybe because, out of all those things,
We are the only ones made in His image
We used 2 live for hundreds of years
But God moved back the line of scrimmage

Because of sin,
This limited the lifespan of men
And now, we are only living 70 or 80 years
And those years are filled
With blood, sweat, and tears

So, we all
Have 2 make the most of our dash,
And it's not about material things
Living that fast life, cars or cash

It's about your relationship with God
And whose life U helped 2 make better
When times 4 them were hard
And they were going through stormy weather

And whom did U help 2 heal
From their emotional scars
This life we live is real
And sometimes, we get real close, but no cigar

Our experiences are like school
We pay the cost 4 every loss until we take
Our last breath, then we wait 2 graduate
But before we get our diploma,
God will ask what did U do with your dash
That time between your birth date and the death date

I Have a Heart Problem

I met a beautiful Queen today
In the lobby at work
She first saw me from a distance and
Complimented my appearance,
My suit, my shoes, my tie, and my shirt

Our spirits spoke 2 one another
I was with my sister, Nina Purple
Who had bought flowers 4 her brother

And we both took a moment and spoke
With this beautiful Queen
With the biggest and beautiful brown eyes
I had ever seen

She was sitting, holding her cane
I asked her, what was her name
And she said, "Cherone"
I could never forget that because
Both my father and my brother's names
Were Jerone

She went on 2 say that
She had a problem with her heart
I looked at her and said,
"You've always had a problem with your heart"

U love hard and give the shirt off your back
You're the shoulder everyone leans on
It's because God built U like that

U have been the go 2 4 so many people
Who have had issues and needed your help
2 solve them
And the reason why is because
God gave U a heart problem

The Best of Blaq Ice

See, she was at the hospital
Because of her physical condition
But God sent her there 4 our encounter
And 2 strengthen her spiritual condition

U got this Queen
Because U are the daughter of a King
He's a healer and a restorer; so, 2 him,
A heart problem is a small thing

So, let that same mind be in U
That was in Christ Jesus
God will never leave U nor forsake us
Because He loves us 2 pieces

So, hold your head up
And straighten your crown
Be steadfast in prayer, strengthen your faith
With a test comes a testimony
May the Lord bless U and keep U
And shine His light upon your face

I Get the Picture

My wife sent me a photo yesterday
Of 4 couples, including her and I
Before she could text a word of her purpose
4 sending it, I immediately understood why

Out of all the couples,
We are the only ones still together
Man, I wish we could do better
I wish we could learn 2 weather

The storms
The bible says, "God prefers us
2 be cold or hot, not lukewarm"

So, be all in or not
U could be wasting someone's time
Or taking someone else's spot

I wish my friends could have made it
I also pray that God sustains mine
That photo was a big wake-up call
Like God sent us a sign

U have 2 learn 2 forgive
I don't care how much it hurts,
And do what U have 2 do
2 make it work

See, love keeps no record of wrongs
That's written in the scripture
I understand why it was meant 4 us
2 see that photo
I get the picture

Don't U Ever . . .

Don't U ever think
That U are not good enough!
This situation has been rubbing U
The wrong way
But, intense rubbing is how U get a buff

U are about 2 shine
U are this close 2 your blessing
And it can come at any time
That's why U have 2 keep your mind

Sharp
The devil is a liar,
He wants 2 knock U off the straight path
Until U expire

But God got a plan A and B
That's why Jesus died on Calvary
So that he could save U and me

And if he could do that 4 us,
What makes me think that we
Won't have 2 pay a fee?

See, we have 2 bear our own cross
Although, sometimes it's not even our fault
You've been riding in the same boat,
And the seas of life got U tossing

And turning
It's a very expensive lesson
But trust me, U are learning

God is humbling U
U've been feeling like the Jones' Girls
Who I can run to

De'Andre Hawthorne

Escape, I know U just want 2 run away
God allowed a situation 2 exist
That would test your faith, take some time
Go in that closet, close the door, and pray

Don't U ever think that
Things have gone on so long
That U can't turn it around
It's never 2 late 2 fix what's wrong

God will give U the strength
2 be strong
Just know that U are not alone

Although the devil
Got U feeling isolated,
U will look back on this moment one day,
And say 2 yourself, "I made it"

So, don't U ever give up
Don't U ever quit
Don't U ever give up hope
Girl, U got this

The Damage Has Been Done

You've been dealing with the same abuse,
Whether physically or verbally,
That tongue is a 2-edged sword
And it cuts so deep, it's like surgery

Although U thought
That things would change,
They didn't even stay the same

They've gotten worse
Now, U do like that song say by Erika Badu,
"Carry around all this baggage
In your purse, BAG LADY"

And it's gotten so heavy
Never before have U been so ready 2 leave
But the closer U get 2 the door,
He pulls something else out of his sleeve

He gives U everything he thinks U want
But nothing that U need
He disguises himself very well, but doesn't
Realize that U can read

Between the lines
4 far 2 long, you've been ignoring the signs
Hindsight is 20/20, and U are wondering,
"How could I have been so blind?"

How could I have wasted
So much time
But this was all by
God's design

It's enough 2 make U numb
The devil's been attacking your self-esteem,

De'Andre Hawthorne

And you've been feeling like
You've been so dumb

U lash out and cut with your tongue
And there is nothing more deadly
Than a woman scorned, U better run

THE DAMAGE IS ALREADY DONE

The Bible says that it's better 2 be
In a corner of a rooftop than 2 deal
With the mouth of a woman in a wide house
The brothers out there
Know exactly what I'm talking about

But we have 2 take responsibility
She's become the Frankenstein we created
Not that same pretty little girl we first dated

She's become a mirror of U
Now, U don't like what U see anymore
But she's a reflection of U

So, now U are both detached emotionally
U are in protection mode
No one wants 2 totally give in
No one wants 2 fold

At this point, only God knows
If this thing can ever be mended
I only wonder
How much could have been prevented
Now U are left with 2 choices
Start all over from scratch or end it

THE DAMAGE HAS ALREADY BEEN DONE

Above the Shoulders and Beneath the Waist

They say that men are from Mars
And women are from Venus
This is not just about gender,
Vaginas, and penises

It's more about the way we think,
And it doesn't matter whether we are
Younger or older
Men are led by what's beneath their waist
And women are led by what's above their shoulders

Whether emotional or physical,
It's been proven, it's statistical
The Egyptians and Greeks made it mythical
It's talked about in Proverbs, it's biblical

A woman could
Look past all your faults
No matter how many times
U broke her heart and got caught

But a man can't stand the thought
Of his woman with someone else
I've had dreams about it,
And woke up pissed off

And was actually mad, now that's real bad
When you're mad at something
That didn't even happen,
Just a figment of your imagination
Just imagine the reaction if it really happened

I think we both expect more
Once we get pass the initial attraction
Women will fall 4 words 4 a minute
But they'd better be backed up by actions

De'Andre Hawthorne

And after men get past her beautiful face,
Fake booty, fake eyelashes, and weave
No matter how fine U are, he will walk away
In a heartbeat 4 his peace

We love y'all, without U
We know it's impossible 4 reproduction
Everything would have been much better
If when He made the woman 4 us,
She would've come with instructions

I guess God made us so different
4 a reason, and it was 4 more than just
Pleasing one another
I'm talking about the easing

Of the mind when times
Are tough and rough
A woman just got the right stuff
2 comfort us

So although we are made different,
We both have our place
Even if a woman is led by what's above her shoulders
And men are led by what's beneath his waist

The Foul-Mouth Christian

I don't know what the hell
U were thinking about
4 someone who's supposed 2 be holier
Than thou, U sure as hell have a foul mouth

Talking about,
"I don't like your spirit"
Well, it's something real funny about yours
Whenever I'm near it

But that's fine
I know that I'm one of a kind
But 2 actually approach me about it,
U must have lost your damn mind

That was the day
Your mind went on vacation
Now, I don't know what's going on in your
Personal life, but whatever U are facing

It ain't got nothing 2 do with me
But I know U, see people like U
Like 2 bully people
Who U think are an easy

Target, messing with me
Let's see how far U get
I hope U don't get tired or lethargic
Cause U ain't never dealt with a brand
Like this, I'm a whole different market

Plus, I'm an artist
So, I can think of many creative ways
4 U 2 hate me
But I chose the positive route, looking good

De'Andre Hawthorne

And U can't stand the sight U see
But you're mad at the wrong person
It was God who made me

So, don't ever try 2 test my manhood, understood?
I'm just a little black boy from the hood,
And I know U would try 2 get everyone
2 hate me if U could

U look at me as if 2 say,
"What good could come out of Englewood?"
Well, my neighborhood has produced greats like
Dubceez, Redski, D Rose, and J Hud

These are only a few
Who I will mention
I know y'all have one of these people at work
I call them the

FOUL-MOUTH CHRISTIANS

We Celebrate U Today

Ms. Tom, we thank U so much
4 being a loving person and a good leader
And awesome colleague, a woman of God
And a believer

I have personally experienced
Your kind spirit
U extend a hand 2 your entire staff
And give good advice 2 those who
Are willing 2 hear it

So on behalf of all us
And your entire Stroger team,
Continue 2 be a good example of leadership,
Continue 2 be creative and continue 2 dream

We celebrate U today
On this national holiday
May God bless U 2 see many many more
Happy Birthday!

De'Andre Hawthorne

That's My Cousin

I don't know what it was about the block
I grew up on
Although I was birthed in Englewood
84th and Carpenter is where I was born

Back then, I had some real true friends
Whom today I call my brothers
I have a few sisters 2
And also a few mothers

We would always crack jokes
On one another and play the dozens
Mommas were always off limits,
And we would be lying our asses off
Talking about

THAT'S MY COUSIN

Let it be somebody that's real popular,
And someone brings up their name
It's like U have 2 make the connection
4 some kind of neighborhood fame

So, U would say,
That's my cousin
2 seal the deal,
And the normal reaction U would get
Is a smile and a
"That's your cousin for real"

Then U double down on the lie,
Talking about, "yea,
That's my cousin on my daddy side"
Knowing deep down inside U are lying

But some of us wasn't buying it
We would cross our arms, lift our heads,
And twist our lips
If your reputation proceeded U,
We already knew U were a trip

I look back on those days,
And laugh,
Just thinking about all those
Good times we had

Man, U couldn't beat those memories
If U played percussion
We were some tripped-out kids
Growing up,
Talking about

THAT'S MY COUSIN

De'Andre Hawthorne

A Moment 2 Remember

It was Sunday January 28, 2024
The time was about 6:45 am
As I walked out the door

Got inside of my telluride
My wife, by my side
We were heading 2 Minnesota from the Chi
Which was a 6 hour-ride

Today was the day
When I was going 2 surprise my Godmother
It's been about 3 long years
Since we've last seen each other

Now, let me give U the back story
On March 1, 1993 at 4:30pm
I began my career at Oak Forest Hospital
Now, I've never been an irrational man
I've always been logical

So, although I began working
4 someone else
About 6 months later, I opened my first
Business and started working 4 myself

I remember walking in the halls of my job,
Selling jewelry with a cold sale's pitch
That's when I met this Queen, named Mary Ford
And we instantly clicked

She began calling me her Godson,
Advised me and protected me,
And whenever I would have a problem
I would run 2 her

The Best of Blaq Ice

She didn't let nobody bother me
I don't care who it was
Whether it was a manager or an employee,
Didn't nobody mess with me

As we got older, she retired
And moved 2 Hammond Indiana
It was her and her son
We would always talk and reminisce
On the good ole days, those times were fun

Then, all of a sudden I could reach her
She was admitted to the hospital,
And her son was the power of attorney
He spoke 4 her

While in the hospital
Come 2 find out, her son died
Shortly after, she was put in a facility,
Not being in her right mind

I looked 4 her 4 a whole year
And couldn't find her
I just hoped that wherever she was,
They were being nice and kind 2 her

Finally, about a year ago, I received a call
Her Goddaughter and her were on the line
It was so good 2 hear her voice
After being absent from each other's lives
All this time

Then on Sunday, January 28, 2024,
I drove from Chicago 2 Minnesota
And surprised her when I walked
Through the door,

De'Andre Hawthorne

This was a moment I will cherish
4 the rest of my life
And right by my side
Was my incredible wife

I greeted her with a poem
We hugged, we cried, we shared a moment
From the heart
Then after that, I had one more surprise
I took her 2 see the house that Prince built,
The historical Paisley Park

I couldn't have planned this day any better
The drive was smooth; the weather, nice
We spent some quality time together
I will never forget it 4 the rest of my life

13 Years Ago Today

Where were U 13 years ago today?
I remember that day
Just like it was yesterday,
And just like that day, today

I wrote a poem about it
It was the greatest snowstorm
I had ever witnessed
All traffic had 2 be rerouted

The place was Chicago, the year was 2011
It was Tuesday, February 1st
I wasn't around during the storm of 1967
But of all the snowstorms I've seen,
This was the worst

I remember opening my front door
And was greeted by snow up 2 my shirt
Digging my car out
So I could try 2 go 2 work

Y'all know that hospitals are never closed
So, I was going 2 do my best 2 drive
Besides, I only worked 20 minutes away
Hospitals operate 7 days a week and 365

I remember the nurses
Staying overnight because they couldn't leave
I remember calling my friend Ria
And telling her 2 stay off of LSD

The cars on Lake Shore Drive were stranded
4 about 3 days; so, I'm glad I paid attention
When I called her, she couldn't believe it
But I was so glad she listened

De'Andre Hawthorne

It took me about an hour 2 get 2 work
When it normally took 20 minutes
Slipping and sliding
Man, I regretted that I was in it

But, I was thinking about my co-workers
Because I really care
And do U know, when I finally made it,
Almost everyone called off?
I was damn near the only one there!

I remember thinking
The good thing about this day was that
There were no crimes. It had 2 be God's will
The murder rate was zero in Chicago
That day, nobody got killed

I will never forget Tuesday, February 1, 2011
That was the day when God opened the sky
And rained down snow from heaven

13 YEARS AGO TODAY

Paisley Park

Growing up in the 80's, there were 2 artists
Who stood above, and left such a footprint
The King of Pop, Michael Jackson
And his Royal Badness, Prince

Well, on Sunday, January 28, 2024
I experienced a moment of a lifetime
I visited Paisley Park where albums
Were created like Signs of The Times

Around the world in a day
Man, if these walls could talk
I wonder what they would say

We were able to see his studios,
His gold and platinum albums on the walls,
His chill rooms and the memories
Of the moments he shared
With other great artists in the halls

I was soaking it all in
Back in the day, when I had no one 2 talk 2,
Prince's music was like my best friend
His music would take me places
I've never been

The sadness of "Another Lonely Christmas",
The energy of "Baby, I'm a Star",
The sensuality of "Do Me, Baby"
It was his voice, his lyrics, and the sound
Of him playing the guitar

He was one of the greatest inspirations
Behind my poetry, like none other

De'Andre Hawthorne

The way I write, using numbers 4 words
I got all of that from reading his lyrics
Inside his album covers

There will never ever be another Prince
He left a vacancy that will never be filled
He will truly be missed
2 Prince, your legacy is already sealed

Celebrating a King

We've come a mighty long way
From the struggle of those who came before us,
Those who left a legacy and built a whole movement
Based on unity and trust

We had each other's backs,
And when they tried to make us sit on the back of the bus,
We boycotted for 381 days
That's how we responded back

We protested in peace,
Turning the nightmare into a dream
With the non-violent resistance principles
Of Mahatma Gandhi
Which gave birth to our beloved freedom fighter,
Dr. Martin Luther King

Oh, but Dr. King was not just a dreamer
He was so much more
It was Dr. King and the Civil Rights leaders who forced
The passing of the Civil Rights Act of 1964

Back then, we organized to get things done
Community meetings, word of mouth, flyers,
And landline phones
There wasn't any social media back then
No internet, and definitely no iphones

Although we were successful in passing new laws,
There would still be obstacles and brick walls
Preventing us from gaining success
In some areas we still couldn't win
We could have the same degrees, the same experience
But the biggest obstacle was the color of our skin

De'Andre Hawthorne

Today, it's time that we rebuild the dream
We have in the legacy
Left by Dr. Martin Luther King

We still have time to make a difference,
And it doesn't matter how strong the resistance,
Change starts right here, right now

Together, we will break
The generational curse,
And when U experience problems in your life,
Like Dr. King,
Have faith in God that He will make it work

Black child,
U can be anything U want 2 be,
A doctor or a nurse

A teacher or a lawyer
Just get in the car, turn the key, start the engine,
Follow the example of our great leaders, like
Kenny Lewis of Kenny's Ribs and Dusties,
James Mattz, and his team of Brokers

Bro. James have been on this journey for years,
Creating a movement that's unstoppable
He is an example for young black men
Because if he can do it, then they know it's possible

So, as leaders, we have no choice
And we have no voice,
Unless we come together in unity
And like Mr. Mattz, we must have a heart,
Filled with concern 4 the black community

So, call on God, in the name of Jesus
With the faith of the prophets and Methusalem

The Best of Blaq Ice

Mr. James Mattz, we thank U 4 being obedient
2 your calling
And like Nehemiah, accepting the assignment of
Rebuilding Chirusalem

Like Dr. King,
U 2 can download your own dream,
Upload faith, believe in yourself,
Create generational wealth

And when the haters try to stop U
And block your dreams
Like Dr. King, don't respond in kind
Build U a firewall,
Monitor and control your mind

We've got some difficult days ahead
But it doesn't really matter now
Because I've been 2 the mountain top,
And I've looked over
And I've seen the promised land

It's time we roll up our sleeves and go 2 work
Together, we will make the dream real
Just remember, people may forget what U say
But they will never forget how U made them feel

2 be honest, I'm tired of talking about it
It's time 2 be about black excellence
In every aspect, shade, and expression,
Greatness and all of the above
Because a life of sacrifice
Is what true leaders and legends are made of

De'Andre Hawthorne

Why Is Our History Offensive?

2 all my white friends and followers:
"Why is Black History so offensive?"
Of course, this doesn't apply 2 every
Woman or man, I'm just trying 2 understand

Why is it, when we talk about our past hurts,
Slavery, segregation and Jim Crow,
Some of U take the position that we should
Get over it, let it go, that was a long time ago?

But we still suffer from the effects
Of what your ancestors did
U can't even fathom
Your mother being raped, your father being
Killed or some strangers coming 2
Take away your kids

This is how my great grandparents lived
Notice, I said my grandparents, parents
I met them, they were still alive
When I was a child
So, although U may think it's been a while

For me, that was just 4 generations ago
And yeah, I know, it had nothing 2 do with U
But many of U reap the benefits
And have no clue

As 2 how U were born into financial stability,
This country was built by the blood,
Sweat, and tears of my ancestors
Many of your banks invested
In the same slave plantations
That enslaved my ancestors

The Best of Blaq Ice

Banks like Citibank, Bank of America and
Wells Fargo, look it up, it's factual
Even J.P. Morgan and Chase apologized 4
Owning slaves, accepting slaves as loan collateral

So, the next time U do your banking,
Get that loan 4 that car or house
U are still benefiting off the blood of my ancestors,
And that's why I can't stop talking about it

Our history
So, I proudly raise my black fist
We may not have videos or many photos
Of what happened but that doesn't mean
It didn't exist

And just 2 be clear,
We don't blame any white person today
4 what happened yesterday
But the legacy of America is here 2 stay

And when U want 2 say, "stop talking about it,
It wasn't our fault,"
Keep that same energy
And say that 2 the victims of the Holocaust

Everyone can talk about their tragedy, but us,
From Black Wall Street
2 the back of the bus,
We've lost trust in this government

A long time ago
But I understand, guilt makes U defensive
Deep down inside U realize what your
Ancestors did, that's why
Our history is offensive

Another Blessing

Good evening, Queen,
I bring U greetings from a young King
I wanted 2 take the time 2 congratulate U
Because of U many students dare 2 dream

I just wanted 2 thank U 4 your service
I remember when we first met
I was on stage hosting that night
U approached me and was like, "Blaq Ice,
I'm Lucille, and I'm cousins with your wife"

That night was real nice
I loved your energy and your smile
I can tell that U had the right mindset,
And I can bet it started when U were a child

Look at U now?
God blessed U with another year
I'm so glad that I made it
And I could be there

2 share in such a beautiful celebration
I bet U are one of the ones God brags about
Among his creation
U are the manifestation

Of our grandparents' dreams
And the vision 4 this family they had in mind
I only wish they could see the legacy
They passed down through their bloodline

So, celebrate the blessings
Of another year of life,
Learning from the mistakes of the past
And making the wrongs right

The Best of Blaq Ice

Take advantage of whatever
Life has in store
Happy Birthday Lucille and may God bless U
2 see many many more

De'Andre Hawthorne

6 Is the Magic Number

6 years ago today,
I was filled with so much joy
My grandbaby came into the world,
8lbs and 13oz, a beautiful baby boy

Christian Price Jr.,
Half Mexican, half Black
I knew that this was just what my son needed
2 stay on track

I watched my son as he held his son
He was so gentle 2 the touch
I heard him say 2 CJ over and over again,
"I love U so much"

He was my superbowl baby
He was born on Super Bowl 52
The Patriots defeated the Eagles
For me, it was like deja vu

I remember when my son was little too,
Picking him up in my arms,
Wanting 2 protect him from
Any danger, hurt or harm

I'm your dad, so as the years passed,
I watched him father his son,
Deal with the challenges of an autistic child
He didn't pack up and run

The doctors said my baby wouldn't talk
That he would only speak in the language of sign
But God has opened his vocal cords
And now he talks all the time

The Best of Blaq Ice

Look at God!
Don't tell me things are 2 hard
Just keep your faith
And let that man upstairs do his job

My CJ is 6 today, there are a few challenges
But the therapist taught him some useful tools
He's very advanced on his Ipad and computer,
And he's doing really good in school

So, 2 my grandbaby,
I'm sending some extra love today
Your Paw Paw loves U,
Happy Birthday!

The Grammys and Jigga

Last night was Grammy night
There were a lot of big moments but the biggest
Moment 4 black social media was Jay Z's speech
Some compared him 2 Kanye when he
Caused a lot of heat

By saying Beyonce deserved an award
Over Taylor Swift
As if 2 say, between the 2,
That Beyonce had the better gift

Or at least the better video
So, when Jay got up there and began 2 speak
They were like, "here we go again"

Jay Z was receiving the Dr. Dre
Global Impact Award
But when he opened his mouth 2 speak
What came out was a double-edged sword

Jay went on 2 say that
The Grammy metrics don't add up here
"How can one artist win the most Grammys ever,
But never for the best album of the year?"

I can tell his message was more geared
Towards the up and coming artist and the youth
He went on 2 say, he was a little nervous
But when he's nervous, he tells the truth

He also said that the Grammys were
Subjective and opinion-based
What he would say next
Would shock the whole place

The Best of Blaq Ice

He said, "after tonight, some of U will feel robbed
And some of U will get robbed,
And some of U don't belong in a category"
U can tell he wasn't there 4 the fame or the glory

In his own words, he said
"We love U, we just want U 2 get it right"
This will go down in history
As one of the best speeches said on Grammy night

See, as a fellow artist, I understand
That whether or not U get the nod of approval by man,
U have 2 keep pushing, keep going,
Invest in your craft, keep growing

And U are guaranteed 2 go far
Just know, whether U ever receive an award or not,
2 your fans and supporters, U will always be a star

Black History Didn't Start with Slavery

U can trace our history back 2 the
First man and woman, Adam and Eve
2 some this may be hard 2 believe

Because in most of the books
They depict Adam and Eve as white
But historical facts and genetics show
That this isn't right

According to the Mendelian Law,
The geneticist Mendel said that it was impossible
4 whites 2 produce blacks
He went on 2 spit out a few scientific facts

Light hair, light skin, and light eyes are recessive
Dark skin, dark hair, and dark eyes are dominant
U can't get the dominant from the recessive
But U can get the recessive from the dominant

This means that Black history
Is the beginning of all history
No matter who U are or where U are from,
It's not a mystery

Just do the research!
Black people built great civilizations
Study the history in your museums
From the great pyramids of Egypt
2 the Roman coliseums

Just about all the Greek fathers studied in Africa
Plato studied for 11 years, Aristotle studied for 13,
Hypocrates and Pythagoras studied for over 20 years,
And Socrates studied for 15

The Best of Blaq Ice

Long before slavery, we were teaching the world
They were learning from us and teaching their people
That's why I can't understand how the white man
Didn't look at us as equals

Who's greater, the student or the teacher;
The prophet or the preacher?
All I'm saying is, although we understood our greatness,
We were humble enough 2 share our knowledge

Opened up the doors of our college
At the Temple of Waset
We gave enough wisdom 2 the world
That for the next 3000 years
There would be enough knowledge 2 last until the internet

Was presented,
And the whole world has benefitted
From all our advances and the things we invented

We were known for our wisdom,
Our great kings, our warriors, and bravery
Black history is the beginning of all history
Black history didn't start with slavery

The Royal Bloodline

My people who are called by my name,
We've all heard or read this before
But I have a question, "who are these people,
And what is his name?"

What does this have 2 do with African Americans
And our ancestral bloodline?
If we just took the time 2 do the research,
There are a few interesting things we will find

Well, let's take a moment and investigate
Let's see where the rabbit hole leads
And how far it takes us

Throughout scripture
Let's go precept upon precept, line upon line
Here a little, there a little, until we get the picture

If U are alive today,
This means that U belong 2 the family
Of one of Noah's 3 sons
But the question is, "which one
Does the African American come from?"

Let's start our journey
In the book of Genesis Chapter 10,
Here we will find
The genealogy of all men

Verses 2 through 5 talks about Japhet's seed
When we see who the children of Japhet are today
We find that the African American doesn't belong
2 none of these

These were all Europeans
And their surrounding isles

See, in the Bible, whites from Europe
Were the only ones considered "Gentiles"

I'm talking about Germans,
The British, the French, and Spanish,
The Slavs, Iranians, Russians and Ukrainians,
Greeks, even the Chinese, and several other
Nations who live on the European plains

This eliminates one out of the three
"So, where are we in history?"
Let's move over 2 Noah's other son, Ham
And shake his family tree

Now, we know that everyone who came
From Ham are the African nations, like
The Egyptians, the Lybians,
The Ethiopians and the Canaanites

There's something about Ham
U all should know
According 2 the Zondervan Bible Dictionary,
Ham is the progenitor of the dark races,
Not the Negroes

Oh, oh!
This means that out of all the African nations,
We don't belong 2 any of them
There is only one son of Noah remaining,
And his name is Shem

This is where it becomes interesting
Through the lineage of Shem and his generations,
We get down 2 the Hebrew Abraham,
And through him, U get 3 different nations

There are the Arabs through his first-born Ishmael
And through Isaac's son came the Israelites

De'Andre Hawthorne

When God adopted his son Jacob
Then the people who are in the land today,
They are Edomites from Esau, the one whom God hated

So, since we are not in the land,
Esau couldn't be our man
This leaves Jacob and the Israelites
So, let us understand

If U are looking 4 a suspect in a line-up,
U first would have 2 pay close attention
I'm sure there would be some similarities
But U would have 2 fit the description

So, let's go over 2 Deuteronomy 28,
Verses 15 through 68
In all those verses,
The talk is about the Israelites and the curses

Hold up, don't get nervous!
We are almost through
Let's look at a few of these curses,
And see whom they apply 2

It would have 2 be a people,
Who were taken from their land,
Scattered and enslaved
Their women would be raped
Their children would be bought, sold and taken away

They would be oppressed by a people
Whose language was strange
These same people would brand them with hot irons,
And call them by another name

And no matter what neighborhood they would live in,
They wouldn't own the businesses, they would be consumers

Making everyone else's business grow
Every other nationality would be above them,
And they would be the lowest on the totem pole

U can look and compare people all over this earth
The sons and daughter of the TransAtlantic Slave Trade
Are the only people who fit this curse
No matter what land they would be taken 2,
Wherever their feet touched dirt

So, who are the African Americans"
Our survival has been nothing but God since our arrival
No matter what we have been through,
And that's because we are the Israelites of the Holy Bible

If my people who are called by my name
Will humble themselves, pray, and seek my face
Then will I hear from heaven, and heal their land
Now, I can read this verse and understand

That God has been watching our struggle all this time
Because we are the people who are called by His name
We are His Royal Bloodline

De'Andre Hawthorne

This Dude Right Here

As a child, my father would take me
2 visit my cousins on 73rd and Marshfield
These were the days of the
Green Machine Big Wheels

Big Mike was my barber, my hair stylist,
My cousin, and my big bro
He used 2 perm my hair
Y'all remember Sta Sof Pro?

Yeah, I know. That was a long time ago
But Big Mike always wanted me 2 look good
He was one of the stars of Englewood

Very well-respected
Someone who did everything he could
2 share his blessings
With all of his friends in the hood

Imagine giving someone advice
Big Mike went a step further and used his influence
2 give opportunities 2 his family and friends
With a career, with CPS
That would cause them 2 be straight
4 the rest of their lives

I'm not saying, he's perfect
Like all of us, he's made some mistakes
But this dude, right here,
Put food on so many people's plates

See, my grandmother and his grandfather
Were sister and brother
Our parents were so close
Our mothers were like sisters
Our fathers were like brothers

The Best of Blaq Ice

I don't really remember a time in my life
When he wasn't in it
Growing up, we were into our own things
But family is family, get it?

We looked up 2 him as kids
We wanted the things he had
We wanted to do the things he did

So, today, we celebrate U, King,
4 the blessing of 62 years of life
I pray that U keep your faith strong,
And get it right with God

I know it's been hard
You've had haters in your life since the start
Don't let it stress U
Let that man upstairs do His job

And U are gonna be alright
Besides, if U ain't got no haters,
Then there is something U ain't doing right

Enjoy these years, your legacy is set
Through your son and grandson,
And may God bless U 2 see
Many more years 2 come

De'Andre Hawthorne

Who Rode the Redline?

I saw a video today
Of an Asian woman who was revealing
Things about the black community
It was very interesting, and this is what she had 2 say

She said that Asian American businesses
Were being redlined by banks
They were being refused loans, depending on
What area they wanted 2 open up their
Businesses in, and they had white politicians 2 thank

They were not allowed 2 make white money
In white neighborhoods
But as long as they sold 2 black people
In black communities, they were all good

They could get their loans,
Send their children 2 college,
And buy their homes

All off of black dollars

I always wondered why my neighborhood
Seemed 2 be the first community
That every ethnic group would go 2
2 set up businesses there
But if we tried 2 set up a business in their
Communities, we would be denied
The laws are clearly not fair

And it's not OK!
As a matter of fact, it's even hard 4
Black people 2 get a business loan
2 open up a business where we stay

We already know that the same value
Is not placed on black life
She went on 2 say that black people

The Best of Blaq Ice

Actually pay twice

Not only do we pay 4 goods and services
But we pay an even greater cost
When the businesses take black dollars
Back 2 their neighborhoods,
Our black dollars are lost

And gone forever
I'm so glad that someone else of another
Nationality said it, because when we say it
It is never

Taken seriously
They act like we don't see what we see
Like we are delirious
I'm glad I heard it because I've always been curious

I already knew it, but now it's confirmed
So, on this day in black history,
Hopefully you've learned

That racism is alive and well
It's always been there
It may have been hidden
But it never went anywhere

At the end of the day, this all falls under the curse
Written in Deuteronomy 28, Verses 43 through 45
In our own community, we would be at the bottom
And the stranger would be very high

She definitely wasn't lying
I can only imagine what Arabic, Korean,
And every other business U see in black
Neighborhoods were told,
And who else rode the redline

Super Bowl 58 Highlights

Now that the Super Bowl is over,
Let's talk about it
The Kansas City Chiefs pulled it off again
That goes out 2 all my friends who doubted

This win is what U call a repeat
The 49ers went down in defeat
Although they were the odds' favor
They failed 2 meet

The expectation of the oddsmakers
Patrick Mahon was the chiefs' savior
I have 2 admit, that boy is bad
Now, let's talk about Taylor

Every time the chiefs had the ball,
They would cut 2 Taylor Swift
For her millions of fans called "Swifties",
I guess they got a gift

And I can't lie, her boyfriend, Travis Kelce
Carried that team on his back
He refused 2 lose
He wasn't going out like that

Now, we have 2 talk about
The halftime show
My boy Usher did his thing
He put on a hell of a show

I loved the way he represented A Town
It was good 2 see Will I Am, Alicia Keys
H.E.R., Ludacris,
Lil John, and Jermaine Dupree

The Best of Blaq Ice

But we have 2 talk about Jermaine Dupri
His patent leather shoes and Bobby Socks
Man, there are so many social media memes
He got the internet hot

Some said he looked like Cee Lo Green;
Others said he was dressed like Wednesday Addams
I know now he wishes that he had worn
Something different, and those socks . . .
I know he wishes he didn't have them

Big ups 2 Usher
He sang my joint Nice & Slow
Too bad Jermaine Dupri was the most talked about,
Coming out of the halftime show

The end of the game was real tense,
And the overtime had so much suspense
This was a classic case of
Offense vs defense

I enjoyed it,
Along with chilling with the Queen
Sometimes what matters most
Are the smallest things

Patrick Mahon is the truth
On the NFL, he's already put his stamp
Congratulations 2 the Kansas City Chiefs
You are 2024 Super Bowl Champs

Monday Morning Quarterback

This poem has nothing 2 do with football
But everything 2 do with life
I figured that it was a good time 4 me 2 write
This poem, considering the Superbowl was last night

I knew the title would grab someone
I'll be honest, I don't know where half
Of these ideas come from
But when I wake up around 4am,
The creative flood gates open up, I grab my phone
Open up my email drafts, and start tapping my thumb

And begin 2 type
The light bulb comes on,
And I began 2 write

And this morning, this is what hit my spirit
Monday Morning Quarterback
This poem goes out 2 those of U who like 2
Criticize, give feedback, and advice after the fact

As a matter of fact, if U were in the same
Situation, U wouldn't know what to do
But here U are, saying everything thing
U would have done, if it were U

U have figured out all the scenarios,
Every angle and equation
U know exactly how 2 solve the problem
That they were just facing

Talking about, if it were me, lol
Shut the hell up, always running your mouth,
And that's coming from someone who
Don't have a pot 2 piss in, or a window 2
Throw it out

The Best of Blaq Ice

These are your Monday Morning Quarterbacks,
Telling U the best way
2 run the best plays
For something that happened yesterday

You've become an expert
On someone else's problems
And what they could have done
2 solve them

I just want U to keep that same energy
When U are in the hot seat, when U are feeling the heat,
When U make a bad decision or 2
And find out things are not that sweet

Where is all the good advice?
When U are going through,
U seem 2 have had plenty
That's why they say, "hindsight is 20/20"

Many of U act just like that
This poem was dedicated 2 the
Monday Morning Quarterback

De'Andre Hawthorne

The True Definition of Love

Today, let's talk about love,
What it means 2 U VS what it truly is
I know there are many definitions,
Whether it's hers or his

But what is it, really?
Y'all remember when we were
Young and silly
In 6th and 7th grade, talking about
We're in love with Kimberly or Billy

My point is,
Was it love or an emotional feeling,
A kiss, a touch or a hug
Why was it so appealing?

There is a reason why Marvin Gaye
Called it "healing"
U just didn't understand
What exactly U were dealing with

See, the body is made up of all types
Of cells, chemicals and hormones, and
Glands that release pheromones

And U think that this is love

Have U ever been addicted 2 the way
Someone made U feel, like a dope fiend?
That's because the body responds the same
When it releases something called "dopamine"

This reaction comes from pleasure
So, the question is, why is it that what U call love

The Best of Blaq Ice

Never lasts?
U are always talking about your exes
And your past

But love is not supposed 2 die
Then why don't U love your exes anymore?
Let's take a moment and explore

Your definition of love
And your understanding of it are vital
2 truly understand what love is
Let's look in the Bible

For God so loved the world
That He gave His only child's life
This tells us that the true definition of love
Is sacrifice

What are we willing 2 change 4 that one
We say we love?
What are we willing 2 do 4 that one
We say we love?

Sometimes we miss the mark by looking 4
A nice body and good looks,
When the signs and marks of what love is
Are all written right in the book

So, the next time someone says they love U,
U can judge it based on what changes
And adjustments they are willing 2 make,
And if someone doesn't sacrifice 4 U,
Then U already know your place

It's not just about money, it's s about time,
Time 2 think about calling U, texting U,
Spending time with U

De'Andre Hawthorne

And doing something nice
There are 2 things that once U lose
U never get back, that's time and your life

So, time is valuable
And whom U choose 2 spend it with is invaluable

Love is time
Love is life
Love is defined by one word
Love = Sacrifice

Making Noise in My Sleep

Last night, my wife had the nerves 2 say
That I woke myself up because I was snoring
How does she know I wasn't just resting
My eyes, and exploring

My thoughts or imagining myself
Making the sound of a car with a loud exhaust?
Maybe I was deep into a meditation
Of being on a loud motorcycle and got lost

Or flying in a jet whose mode was on stealth
Either way it goes, I know I don't snore
Because if I snore like she says I do
How come I've never heard it myself?

Man, I think my wife be tripping
U know what I really think
She just don't want 2 be up by herself
And she'd be missing me

I've done sleep studies and CPAPs,
Pulled covers way down 2 my knee caps
If I'm cold, I just might sleep with a ski cap,
Close my eyes, think about my day, and do
A recap

But I don't snore!
I'm telling y'all that's a bunch of crap
I might be dreaming about wrestling
The Tribal Chief Roman Reign
At Wrestlemania in a championship rematch

Maybe that's the noise she hears
I'm just not the type who counts sheep
Maybe your husband has a vivid imagination,
And maybe that's why I'm making noise in my sleep

De'Andre Hawthorne

Between a Rock and a Hard Place

I just wanted 2 take a moment
2 encourage U, U got this!
You've been here before
I know right now it feels like U've been
Locked behind closed doors

And there is no way out
Although things look very dark, keep the faith,
Remove the doubt

Just think about it, this ain't the first time
You've been through the storm
I remember it just like it was yesterday
Things were so bad 5 years ago
But look at me today

U will eventually get over and through this
One day, U will look back with a smile
And think about how far U've come
In this journey of life and the many miles

In life. At some point,
Everyone is going to lose some friends
But don't be afraid 2 lose
Because sometimes U gotta lose 2 win

So, once U process everything,
Get over the thought of losing
Don't waste time focusing on the problem
Focus on the solution

A positive outlook determines
A positive outcome
Keep your eyes on the prize
Do U understand where I'm coming from?

Look at the glass as half full,
And not half empty
U are always going 2 have haters
And enemies

We all go through changes, and just maybe,
It's about 2 be your season
So, maybe God placed these bolders
In your life 4 a reason

It's all about opportunity and space
Sometimes the safest place 2 be
Is between a rock and a hard place

A Proper Salute

I would like 2 dedicate this poem
2 the men and women who never get credit
4 the hard work and dedication
That they display on an everyday basis

U have helped 2 heal the broken-hearted
U have helped 2 get many careers started
U have given opportunity 2 several artists

But as soon as they give their list
Of thank yous, somehow they get amnesia
I mean, U have loaned and donated money
Those same people started acting funny

And U are feeling used
But don't get it twisted or confused,
U are not a fool or a tool

There are some people
Who are just built this way
It's a flaw in their character
But they are some really good actors

These are your Bible-quoting Christians,
Your gifted and anointed artists,
Family members, friends and co-workers
U just happen 2 be an easy target

See, U have a big heart,
And U wanna see everybody win
I've seen U treat strangers like friends
And friends like family

But still get admonished
These are some tough learning lessons

The Best of Blaq Ice

That you've had 2 pay a heavy cost 4
Some people pay less
4 an education in college

So, 2 those of U who rarely get acknowledged
By those whom U mentored and invested in
Those whom U have given opportunities
And advice 2, helping them win

God bless U, keep doing your thing
And most of all, don't change
Forgive but don't forget
See, they don't understand

That there will be bigger, better and greater
Opportunities, but this time,
U will remember those who appreciate U
And when it comes 2 who U will give this
Great opportunity 2, U know what 2 do

The moral of the story is,
Don't burn the bridges that got U
From point A to B
Be just as excited as U were
When U received the blessing,
When U are telling the story

About who helped U along the way
And 2 those who are feeling slighted
I know your heart is pure
I wanted U 2 know that we see U
We know what U have done
And whom you've done it 4

U will get your just due in time
Last but not least,
Don't cast your pearls before swine

De'Andre Hawthorne

I just wanted 2 take a moment
2 tell U that U don't have 2 prove anything
Just continue 2 bear good fruit,
And if no one ever says, "thank U",
I just wanted 2 be the one who gives U
A PROPER SALUTE

BlaqIce.com

The Picture Gallery

The Best of Blaq Ice

De'Andre Hawthorne

The Best of Blaq Ice

De'Andre Hawthorne

The Best of Blaq Ice

De'Andre Hawthorne

The Best of Blaq Ice

De'Andre Hawthorne

The Best of Blaq Ice

De'Andre Hawthorne

The Best of Blaq Ice

De'Andre Hawthorne

The Best of Blaq Ice

De'Andre Hawthorne

The Best of Blaq Ice

De'Andre Hawthorne

The Best of Blaq Ice

De'Andre Hawthorne

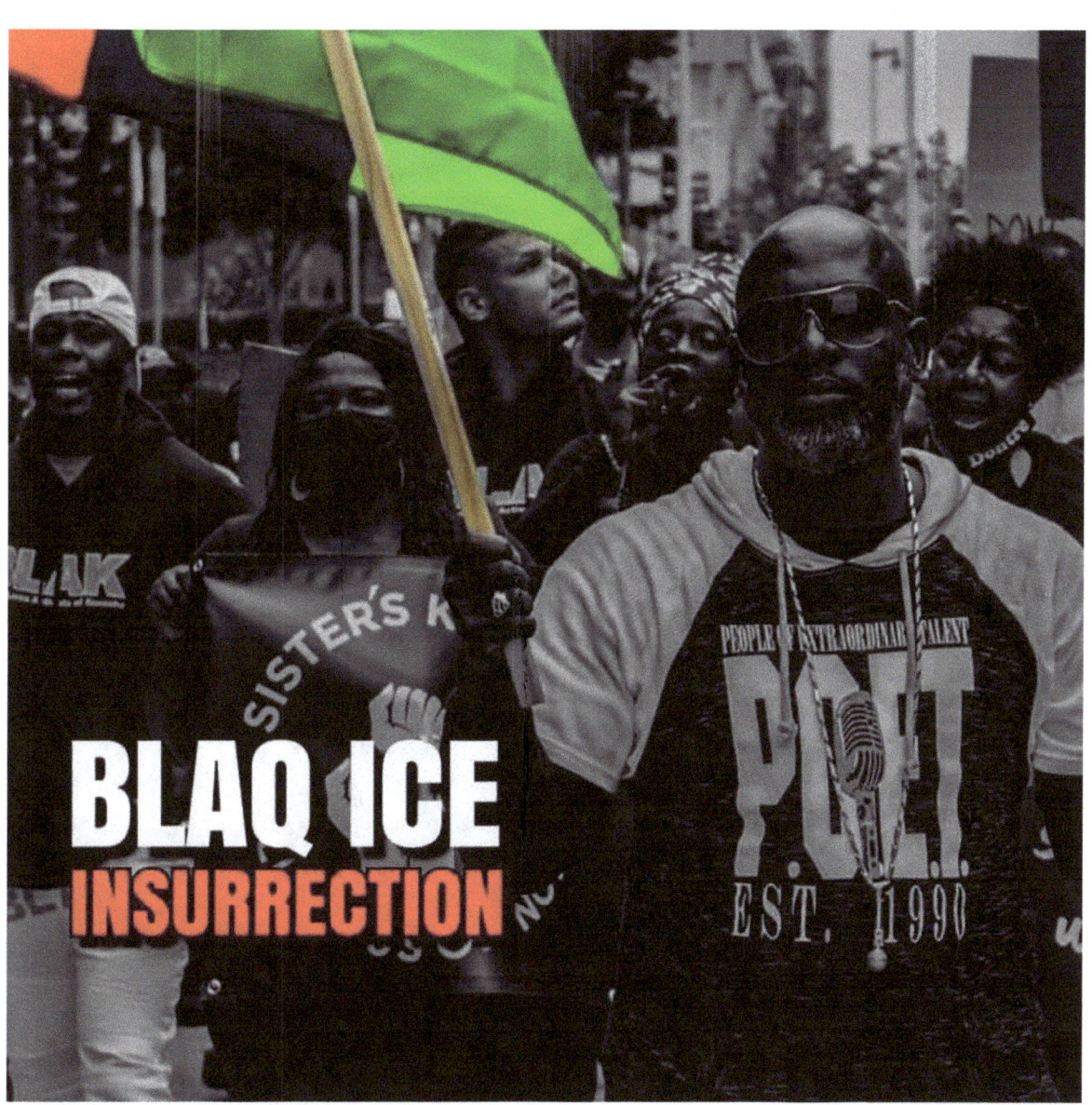

The Best of Blaq Ice

The Best of Blaq Ice

Epilogue

About De'Andre Hawthorne

Once in a generation, society is graced with a visionary spirit that ignites cultural change, redefines greatness, and paves the way for future generations. De'Andre Hawthorne, AKA Blaq Ice, is undoubtedly one of the greatest Spoken Word entertainers of his era. His influence reaches far beyond the realms of arts and entertainment. Through his artist-activist movement, P.O.E.T., Blaq Ice has touched communities across America, empowering thousands to use their talents to make extraordinary contributions in their neighborhoods.

A legend in Chicago's hip-hop community and a tireless activist, the author transforms words into action. His commitment to uplifting others led him to establish the Legends of Chicago Hip Hop in 2013 and the National Spoken Word Awards in 2016, both of which continue to inspire and honor the legacy of those who shape our culture.

BLAQ ICE
De'Andre Hawthorne

De'Andre Hawthorne AKA Blaq Ice is an Award Winning, American poet, International Spoken Word life artist, entertainer, lecturer, promoter, producer, host, videographer, graphic designer, published author, mentor and activist. The contributions of this amazing artist, world-wide and Chicago spoken word poetry is truly Monumental. Blaq Ice travels the world yearly, produces concerts and award ceremonies.

He has performed in front of thousands and has graced some of the biggest stages, such as The Arie Crown Theater, The Horseshoe Casino, The Taste of Chicago, DuSable Museum, The Daley Plaza & the African Fest. In addition, he has featured in some of the historic poetry venues around the nation, such as the Green Mill in Chicago and The Apache Café in Atlanta.

AWARDS

2013 - 2024
10X CHICAGO MUSIC AWARD WINNER

2023
DUBCEEZ ARTIST OF THE DECADE

2018
LANGSTON HUGHES AWARD HONOREE

2017
GAME CHANGER AWARD HONOREE

2013 - 2016
6X NATIONAL POETRY AWARD WINNER

2016
ICON AWARD HONOREE

FILM

2017
STEP OFF THE BLOCK
Currently on Prime Video & Tubi

2014
SEX AIN'T LOVE
Currently on Prime Video & Tubi

2006
WELCOME TO THE SOUTHSIDE
Currently on Prime Video

ALBUMS / BOOKS

- 30 ALBUMS 2003 -2022
- 12 BOOKS AVAILABLE ON AMAZON

PERFORMER

PRODUCER

- WRITER

COMMUNITY

PHILANTHROPIST

ACTIVIST

EXPERIENCE

2017 - Present
NATIONAL SPOKEN WORD AWARDS
CEO & FOUNDER
The National Spoken Word Awards was founded in 2017 by De'Andre Hawthorne aka Blaq Ice. The awards were created to honor American Spoken Word Artists and those international Spoken Word artists who have made an impact in the United States. The 1st annual Spoken Word Awards was held on Saturday September 2, 2017 in Chicago IL. The NSWAs IS held every year, the weekend of Labor Day.

1990 - Present
P.O.E.T (People Of Extraordinary Talent)
FOUNDER
P.O.E.T. People Of Extraordinary Talent was established by Blaq Ice in 1990 in Chicago, IL. P.O.E.T is an artist activist organization that has toured the Chicago Public School System and the City Colleges of Chicago for over 20yrs with anti-drug, anti-gang, motivational and inspirational messages through poetry.

2010 - Present
P.O.E.T Online Radio Station
FOUNDER
P.O.E.T. Radio was founded by De'Andre Hawthorne AKA Blaq Ice in 2010. The Poetry show, "Voices Behind The Pens" airs Mondays at 8pm CST. It is an online open mic that showcases poets all over the country.

2010 - Present
NATIONAL SPOKEN WORD FEST
FOUNDER
The NATIONAL SPOKEN WORD FEST, formerly known as the P.O.E.T UNITY CONVENTION and NATIONAL POETRY FEST CHICAGO, was founded by De'Andre Hawthorne aka King Of Poetry Blaq Ice from Chicago. The fest has been going on since July of 2010.

2003 - 2013
STRICTLY 4 THE LISTENERS OPEN MIC POETRY SET
FOUNDER & CO-HOST
STRICTLY 4 THE LISTENERS was the premier open mic poetry set on the south-west side of Chicago for over a decade. That open mic featured Grammy award winning poets and veteran poets to newcomers.

CONTACT INFO

www.blaqice.com
BLAQ ICE PRODUCTIONS
Phone: 312.719.7310
Email: kingofspokenwordblaqice@gmail.com

www.iampoet.com
P.O.E.T People Of Extraordinary Talent
Phone: 708.267.9725
Email: blaqiceprd@yahoo.com

Web Links

of the

Author

BlaqIce.com

FACEBOOK
Blaq Ice Chicago

X
BlaqIcePoetKing

INSTAGRAM
kingofpoetryblaqice

YouTube
BLAQ ICE TV

TikTok
kingofpoetryblaqice

LinkedIn
KING OF POETRY BLAQ ICE

Inner Child Press International

Inner Child Press is a publishing company founded and operated by writers. Our personal publishing experiences provide us with an intimate understanding of the sometimes-daunting challenges writers, new and seasoned, may face in the Business of Publishing and Marketing their Creative "Written Work".

Publisher Information:

Inner Child Press International

intouch@innerchildpress.com

www.innerchildpress.com

building bridges of cultural understanding

www.innerchildpress.com

you too can become a published author ...